# ReCreating Your Self

By Neale Donald Walsch

Author of *Conversations with God*

Copyright 1995 by Neale Donald Walsch

All rights reserved, including the right to reproduce this
work in any form whatsoever, without permission
in writing from the author, except for brief passages
in connection with a review.

Published by
Millennium Legacies Inc.
PMB #1144
1257 Siskiyou Blvd.
Ashland, OR 97520

Distributed by
Hampton Roads Publishing Company
1125 Stoney Ridge Road
Charlottesville, VA 22902
call: 1-800-766-8009
email: hrpc@hrpub.com
web site: http://www.hrpub.com

If you are unable to order this book from your local
bookseller, you may order directly from the distributor
above. Quantity discounts for organizations are available.

Library of Congress Catalog Card Number: 00 091353
ISBN 0-9678755-1-X
Printed in Canada
10 9 8 7 6 5 4 3 2 1

*Dedicated to*

**Dr. Leo Bush**

*of Casper, Wyoming,*
*whose life has been a*
*demonstration to so many*
*of what it means*
*to walk the higher ground,*
*to seek the grander choice,*
*to speak a gentler word,*
*and*
*to live in positive awareness*
*of the inherent goodness*
*in every person and situation.*

Welcome to one of the most important books you will ever read.

You are about to learn the meaning of Life. You are about to be given the keys to the Universe. You will then be handed the tools with which to fashion the life for which you have always yearned; the life of your dreams.

Your life is about to change, in some very important ways. So is the life of everyone else. *All* of life is changing, everywhere on the planet.

You cannot have missed this. It is happening on every level: political, geophysical, economical, theological, psychological and philosophical. And without understanding the meaning of Life, without holding the keys to the Universe, without possessing the tools with which to fashion your dreams, you will quite likely be at the *effect* of all of these changes, rather than the *cause* of them.

The first thing to understand here is that these are not just pretty words. Your life *is* going to change... *with you or without you.* Life is very impartial. It doesn't care whether you were part of creating change, or just an uninvolved bystander. It gives you the *choice*, of course, but it doesn't care which you choose. It keeps on with its Process, and it does it with you or without you as an active partner.

That's important to remember. Life Goes On, whether you do or not. Which is the first of many principles explored in this book.

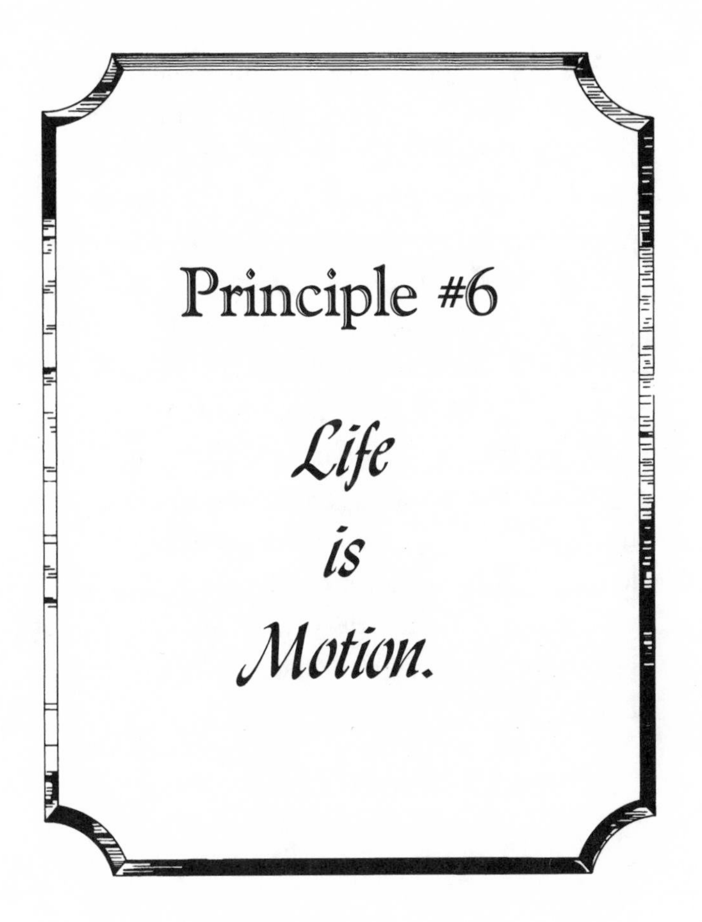

# Principle #6

## *Life is Motion.*

What happened to Principles 1-5?

They are explained in the opening book of this series, *Bringers of the Light*, which may be obtained through the Foundation listed at the back of this publication.

This book has been produced in response to a request from the Foundation for a series of books which break down the wealth of information in *Conversations with God - Book 1*, putting it into the context of practical applications to everyday life. Each book stands on its own, yet each flows into the other in a continuing exploration of the wisdom and understandings in the larger book.

This second in the series deals with the Process of Re-creation, which is, of course, the Process of Life itself.

# What Life is "up to"

Life – that which we call "Life"– is really a Process. It is a Process with no beginning and no end. That is difficult for most people to imagine, for we live in a linear world, with beginnings and endings. Yet *Conversations with God* tells us that in the World of the Absolute, there *is* no Beginning and no End. There simply is All That Is.

All That Is is all there ever was, and all there ever will be. Some people consider that a secret of Life. Yet here is the largest secret: *All That Is* is not a "*thing.*" It is not an Object, a Being, or a Something. It is a Process.

A *process.*

Do you get that? Do you understand that? God is not a *someone* or a *something.* **God is a *process.***

This may be the first truly new idea you've been given about God in a very long time, so think about it.

*God is a Process.* That Process is what we call Life. Therefore: **God is Life.**

And what is Life (God) "up to?" Well, Life is, to borrow from the eloquent genius of Ernest Hemingway, *A Moveable Feast.*

Life is... *moving.* Life is... energy in motion. And it is *always* in motion, not in motion just a little of the time, or part of the time, but *all* of the time.

This helps us to understand an observable fact about Life, which is that Life is always changing. It does not remain the same. How can it if it is *always moving?*

Movement *is* change. Everything which moves changes. If nothing else, it changes *position.* Here, then, is...

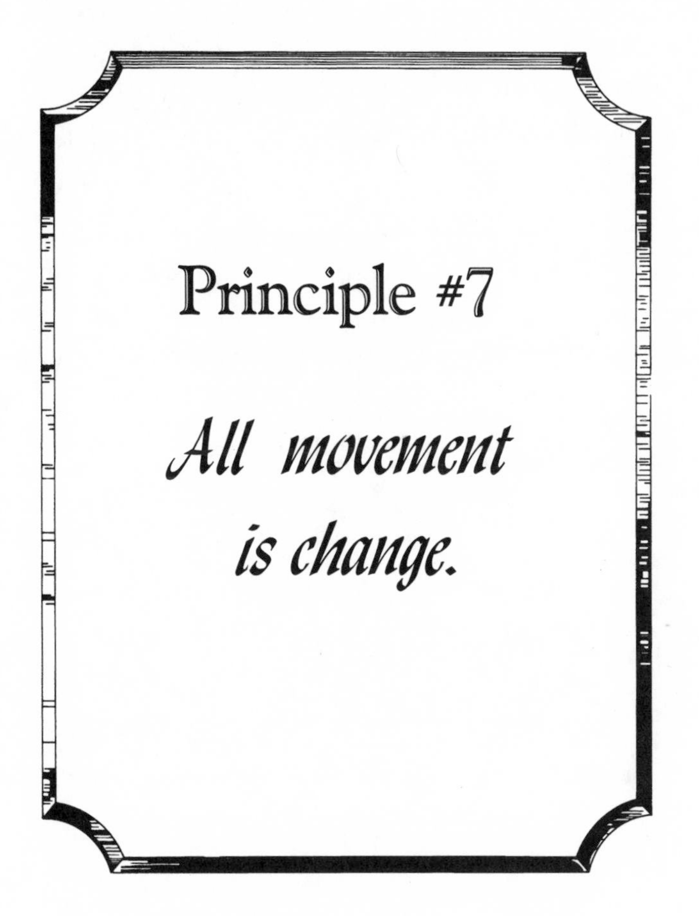

# Principle #7

## *All movement is change.*

If a thing moves, it is not the "same" as it was before. The very act of its movement produces a shift in its very self. Even a change of position is a change of substance, for it is a change of context, and in your life context *is* substance. Put another way, nothing is what it appears to be, taken out of context. In life, position is everything. And the reason *this* is so, is that your position creates your *perspective*.

And perspective creates reality.

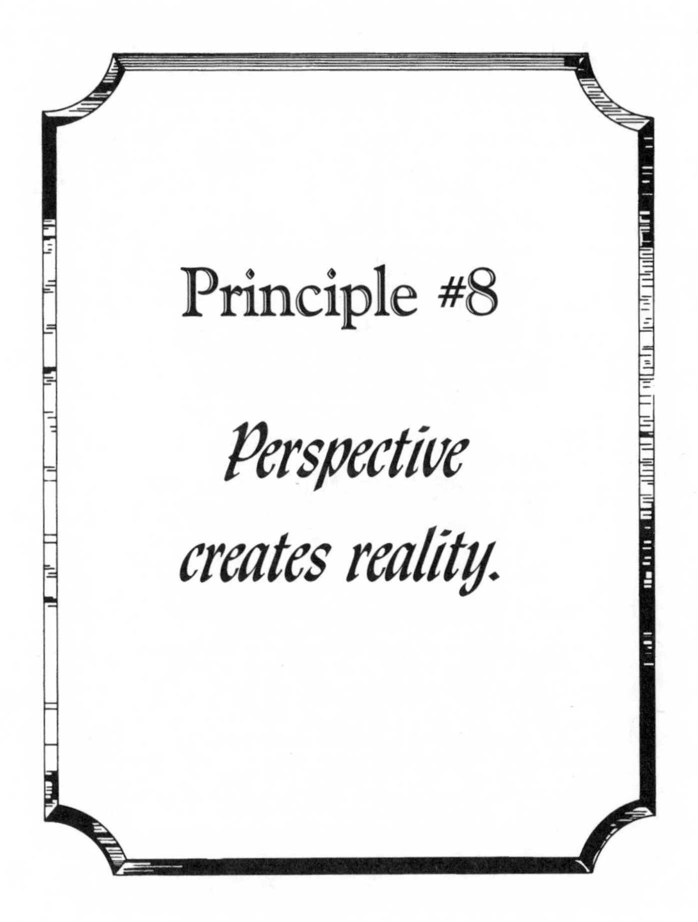

# Principle #8

*Perspective creates reality.*

Things are not what they seem to be. That may very well be the most important thing you'll ever learn. Perhaps you've already learned it. That would be good, because it has no doubt saved you a lot of trouble; a lot of pain.

If one man approaches another man at the mall and gives him a pat on the bottom, the first man may very well react in a negative way.

If, on the other hand, the two men are playing football for the Denver Broncos, it will not matter a bit if one has patted the other on the bottom. In fact, it will matter if he has *not.*

You see, context is everything. Perspective creates reality.

An American couple, visiting in Mexico, was disgruntled because it had rained for three days. The Mexican running their small hotel was happy. "Keeps the dust down," he smiled.

Viewpoint is critical.

# There is no such thing as reality

Now, since things are always moving, the context within which you experience life is always changing. Therefore, perspective is always changing. Therefore, reality is always changing.

Put another way, there *is* no "reality." For if reality is always changing, then what is real?

The answer is: nothing.

That is a profound answer. That is a great truth. That is the ultimate wisdom.

Yet many people find this answer painful. They want things to stay the same, to remain, to go unchanged. And this is the one request the Universe cannot grant. It does not know how. For It cannot be what It is not, and the one thing It is not is that which remains unchanged.

And so, people searching for the Unchanged search in vain.

Desperate is their search, and in their desperation, having been unable to locate anything which does not change in this, their present experience, they look to the heavens, declaring that *God* must be the thing that Does Not Change.

This becomes their anchor, their port in the storm. Yet God is not an anchor, saving you from being carried adrift. God is a *sail*, taking you to the high seas. For that is where the adventure is.

## The cause of pain

Pain is the result of your failure to see this, to understand it, to move with the Rest of Everything. You *will* move, of course, because all of *life* is moving – it cannot *not* move – and you cannot not move, either. But you can try.

This will cause you pain. And it will prove fruitless. For nothing remains static. Nothing goes unchanged. Nothing stands still. Everything moves, all of the time. Allow yourself, then, to go with the flow. Ride the tide. Catch the wave.

You will drown if you do not.

Then the wave will have its way with you.

You see, the wave *will* have its way – you may as well get that straight. It will take you exactly where it is going.

The difference in the quality of your life, therefore, depends directly upon how you answer the next question:

Are you content to simply ride the waves, allowing them to carry you wherever they may go, or do you intend to go where *you* want to go?

If you choose the latter, there is only one way you can create that.

*You* have to be the one *to make waves.*

If you were thinking of being someone who didn't "rock the boat," someone who never "made waves," this book is not for you. Every Master has "made waves." Every one who has mastered life has "rocked the boat." One or two of them have actually opened the floodgates, bringing water to the desert. That is, they have changed life on the planet. They have made an enormous impact.

You, too, will make an impact – and it may very well be enormous – should you undertake to implement the lessons in this book.

This book is about Re-creating Your Self. It is about re-creating yourself in the Grandest Version of the Greatest Vision you ever held about Who You Are.

When you undertake to achieve such an objective, when you move toward such an ideal, when you seek to raise yourself to such a level, you will "make waves." You may as well get used to it. You are going to upset the apple cart. You are going to impact not only yourself, but the lives of other people as well. Because you will be noticed.

You cannot implement the kinds of changes we are talking about here, you cannot recreate yourself in the kinds of ways we are referring to here, and not be noticed.

Every Master is noticed... and we are talking about moving you to mastery.

Are you ready for the journey? Are you prepared for the undertaking? To be so, you must be bold. You must be brave. You must be through – sick and tired, and *through* – with how things have been for you, and willing now, fully and at last, to *seek a newer world.*

Someone once said, there are only three qualities needed for anyone to achieve greatness.

Audacity. Audacity. Audacity.

That someone was correct.

Everything you have read so far is based on a statement that Life is Motion. That statement is supported by unlimited empirical evidence. One can pick anything, anything at all, that one sees in life and, when placing it under a microscope, find that it is composed of tiny particles of matter, *all of them in motion.*

Nothing you see, nothing at all, is *not* in motion. Even that which you do *not* see is in motion. To be sure, *that is exactly why you do not see it.* It is moving so fast, you *cannot* see it!

It is noted, then, that All Things are the Same Thing – simply Energy In Motion. This motion is sometimes called *vibration.* And the *speed* of the vibration is what causes a thing to be "visible" or "invisible" to your eyes. For people who can see things which are moving very fast, *all things are visible.*

It is said that Christ was such a person. And so, too, many other Masters. That is why Masters have always been able to perform apparent miracles. They simply see more.

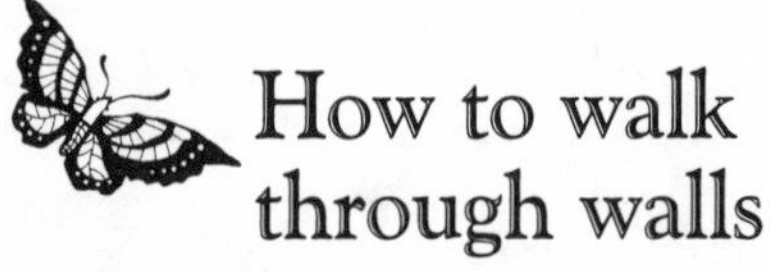

# How to walk through walls

Everyone thinks it was amazing that Jesus apparently walked through walls. Yet Jesus did not think it amazing at all. He simply *looked to see where he was going.*

First, Jesus observed that he, and everything else in Life, was 99.9% *space.* He also observed that the .1% which was Matter was constantly in motion. That is, the particles of Matter were always moving. All he had to do, then, was observe very closely the Matter of which he, himself, was composed...and, literally, *watch where he was going.*

He did exactly the same thing with the Matter of which the wall was comprised. To walk *through* the wall, he simply placed *his* Matter where the *wall's* Matter was not. In other words, he didn't move *through* it at all, he *moved right past it!*

Do you understand this? Do you get what's just been given you? This is a great secret. Do you get it?

This is why, by the way, when you "bump into" some obstacle in your life, people often say, "What's the *matter?*" Indeed, this is a most appropriate question. It is also why, when things are going well, and you are facing no obstacles, you are said to be "in a good *space.*"

Now it will probably be a while yet before you can see things as clearly as a Master. Jesus could literally look into the wall, and into himself, and into everything else in Life, and differentiate between the Space and the Matter. Therefore, he always knew "what was the matter!" And he also knew that 99.9% of the time *nothing was the matter at all.*

This ability to look into an object (or even a Thought – which is simply an Object moving faster), is called *insight.* All people have it to one degree or another, and some people have it to a very high degree. Not many have it to the degree demonstrated by Jesus...but all people *can,* if they *choose to.*

Some people cannot believe this. They cannot believe that they could be given - indeed, that they *have* - the same abilities as Jesus. Yet this level of faith is the key to *experiencing* those gifts.

It was Jesus himself who said, "*According to your faith be it unto you.*" It was Jesus himself who said, "O *woman, great is thy faith: be it unto thee even as thou wilt.*" And the woman's daughter was made whole from that very hour. And it was Jesus himself who said, "*If ye have faith as a grain of mustard seed, ye shall say unto this mountain, Remove hence to yonder place; and it shall remove; and* **nothing shall be impossible unto you.**"

✓ Still, if you cannot believe in yourself and in your own divine heritage (and because so many people cannot), Jesus, in an act of enormous love and compassion, invites you to believe in Him.

✓ "Verily, verily, I say unto you, He that believeth on me, the works that I do shall he do also; and greater works than these shall he do; because I go unto my Father. And whatsoever ye shall ask in My name, that will I do, that the Father may be glorified in the Son. If ye shall ask any thing in My name, I will do it."

Isn't that an extraordinary promise? So great and so complete was Jesus' understanding of who He was, and of who you are ("*I and My Father are one*", He said, and later, "*all ye are brethren*"), that He knew deeply there was no limit to what you could do if you believed in *yourself*, or in *Him*.

Could there be a mistake about Jesus' intentions here? Could there be a misinterpretation? No. His words are very clear. He wanted you to consider yourself One with the Father, exactly as He is One with God. So great was His love for all humankind, and so full was His compassion at their suffering, that He called upon Himself to rise to the highest level, to move to the grandest expression of His being, in order to present a living example to all human beings everywhere. And then He prayed - earnestly prayed - that we would not only see the evidence of *His* Oneness with the Father, but our own as well.

(*"And for their sakes I sanctify* Myself, *that they also might be sanctified through the truth. Neither pray I for these alone, but for them also which shall believe on* Me *through their word; That they all may be one; as thou, Father, art in* Me, *and I in thee, that they also may be one in us: that the world may believe that thou hast sent me.* **And the glory which thou gavest me I have given them; that they may be one, even as we are one.**")

You can't be much clearer than that.

*Conversations with God* tells us that all of us are members of the Body of God, though we imagine ourselves to be separate, and not part of God at all.

Christ understood our difficulty in believing that we were part of God, part of God's very *body*. Yet Christ *did* believe this of *himself*. It was therefore a simple matter (and a marvelous inspiration) for Him to invite those who could not imagine themselves to be a part of *God* to imagine themselves to be a part of *Him.* For He had already declared *Himself* to be a part of God...and if we could simply believe that we were a part of *Christ*, we would by extension *necessarily be a part of God.*

Jesus must have emphasized this point many times, because the record of his teachings, and the commentaries upon them, in the Bible contains countless references to this relationship

String just a few of these separate references together and you have an extraordinary revelation:

*I and my Father are one.* (JOHN 10:30)

*And the glory which thou gavest Me I have given them; that they may be one, even as we are one.* (JOHN 17:22)

*I in them, and thou in Me, that they may be made perfect in one.* (JOHN 17:23)

*That the love wherewith thou hast loved Me may be in them, and I in them.* (JOHN 17:26)

*So we, being many, are one body in Christ, and every one members one of another.* (ROMANS 12:5)

*Now He that planteth and He that watereth are one.* (1 COR. 3:8)

*For we being many are one bread, and one body: for we are all partakers of that one bread.* (1 COR. 10:17)

*For as the body is one, and hath many members, and all the members of that one body, being many, are one body: so also is Christ. For by one Spirit are we all baptized into one body, whether we be Jews or Gentiles, whether we be bond or free; and have been all made to drink into one Spirit.*

*For the body is not one member, but many. If the foot shall say, Because I am not the hand, I am not of the body; is it therefore not of the body? And if the ear shall say, Because I am not the eye, I am not of the body; is it therefore not of the body?* (1 COR. 12-16)

*But now are they many members, yet but one body.* (1 COR. 12:20)

All of us are members of the Body of Christ. All of us are *The Christed One.* And if Christ is one with God, so, too, are we. We simply do not know it. Refuse to believe it. Cannot imagine it.

Now it may seem to you that this book is placing a great deal of emphasis on the teachings of Jesus, and in this section, at least, it obviously is. This extended diversion has been taken because Jesus was one of the greatest, most unequivocal teachers of the Grandest Truth there ever was – and this book is about grand truth.

Yet it is not true that going *through* Jesus is required in order to be going *with* Jesus. Jesus never uttered such words, nor did He come close. That was not His message.

His message was: If you cannot believe in Me, if you do not believe that I am who I say I am what with all that I have done, then you will never, ever believe in Yourself, in who *you* are, and your own experience of God will be virtually unattainable.

Jesus did what He did, performed miracles, healed the sick, raised the dead – even raised *Himself* from the dead – that we might know Who He Was... and thus know also Who WE Really Are.

It is this *second part of the equation* which is most often left out of the traditional doctrine about Christ.

Obviously this is true, for Jesus said He was one

with His Father (whom He identified as God), and He said we were one with Him, and so it follows that failure to believe in Him means failure of the entire construction. The building comes crashing down.

That is a shame, because this is God's building we are talking about (*For we are labourers together with God: ye are God's husbandry, ye are God's building.* 1 COR. 3:9)

Thus we see that we can walk the path together *with* our Master (whoever that Master may be), or we can imagine ourselves to be able to get where we want to go only *through* our Master.

Which shall it be, *with* or *through?*

True Masters invite you to walk the path *with* them to God, that they might show you the way. False masters tell you that you must go *through* them to get to God.

There is a teaching: 'IF YOU SEE THE BUDDHA ON THE STREET; KILL HIM.' The point of the teaching is that if a person declares himself to be the Buddha, appears to be the Buddha, and demands that you follow him because he *is* the Buddha, you'd better watch out, because The Buddha would never do that.

So, too, is it with every Master.

As it is written in *Conversations with God*: "*A true Master is not the one with the most students, but the one who creates the most masters.*"

And, "*A true God is not the one with the most servants, but the one who serves the most, thereby making Gods of all others.*"

So it is possible for all of us to see the movement in everything, and one day perhaps we will. One day we will all have such wonderful in-*sight*. Yet for now it is sufficient simply to know of it. It is sufficient to simply know that Life is Motion. Life is That Which Moves.

The implications of this are astonishing and far reaching, for now we are beginning to come up with a formula:

> Life is Motion.
> All things move.
> God is all things.
> God is That Which Moves.
> All movement is change.

God is, therefore, change...or That Which Changes.

Got it? You have to follow this closely, or you'll lose the thread. Have you got it? Read it again if you have to. Stay with it.

Good.

Now if it is true that...

**God is That Which Changes**

and if it is also true that...

**You are One with God**

then it is *also* true that...

**You are That Which Changes**

And indeed you are. That is all you are doing all the time. Changing.

You are...the "*Changling.*"

Which brings us to...

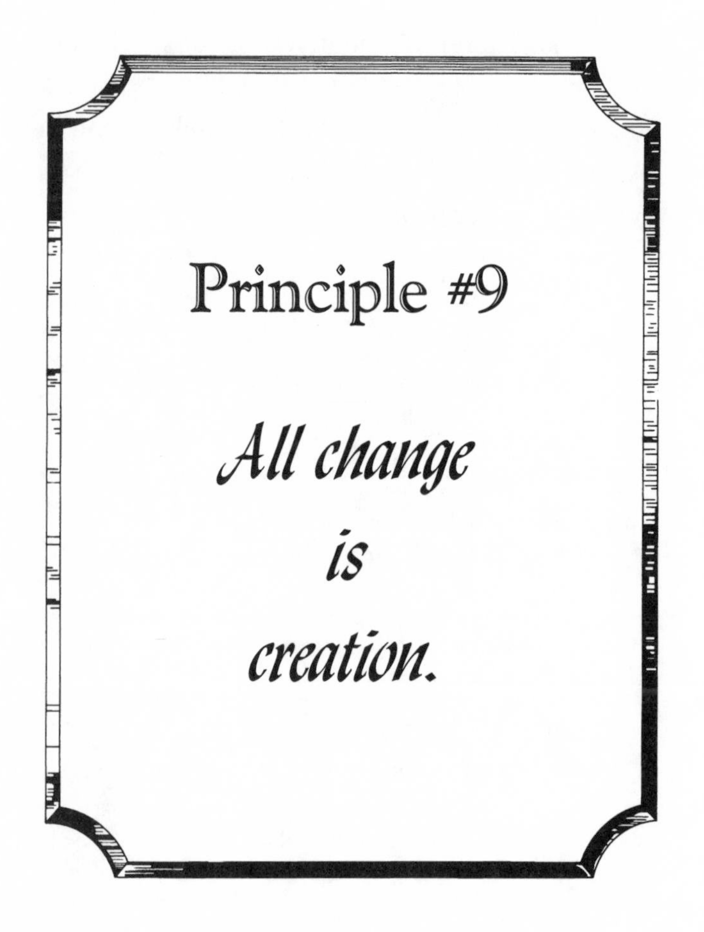
Principle #9
All change
is
creation.

This book has gone to great lengths to make this point. It has moved in circular directions, going over much of the same ground in different ways, to bring you back again and again to this same point:

Life – that is, God...that is, *You* – *will constantly change.* It is your nature. It is the nature of *all* things. It is the reason that you cannot begin now to start re-creating yourself. You are already re-creating yourself. From the day you were born (and before), you have been doing nothing else.

Therefore, this book is not about showing you how to recreate yourself, but rather, about opening your eyes to the fact that *you are already doing what you thought this book might show you how to do.*

You already *know* how to "recreate yourself." In fact, you don't know how *not* to. For you are by nature That Which Creates and Recreates.

Yet not knowing *this* will make it impossible for you to create consciously what you choose, for you cannot experience that which you do not know yourself to be, and you cannot do that which you do not think you can do.

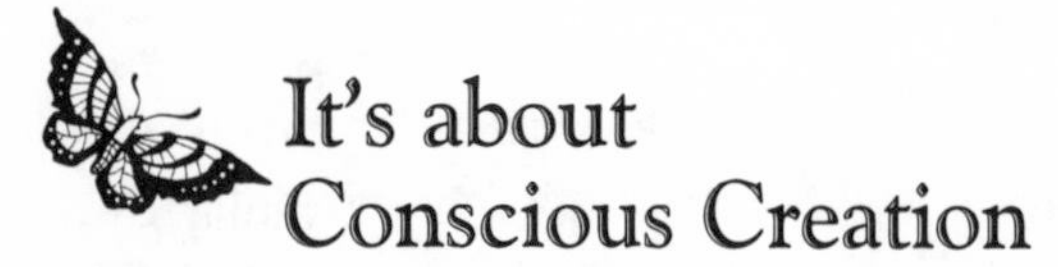

# It's about Conscious Creation

There are many levels of creation. (*Friendship with God* page 115.

All people are creating all the time. The question is not whether they are creating, but whether they are creating *consciously* (that is, specifically choosing what they desire, and calling it forth), or *unconsciously* (that is, simply noticing what they have placed in the space of their own life – and wondering how it got there.)

Knowing and truly understanding what has just been said here will allow you to take an enormous step in your evolution. For if Principle #9 is correct (and it is), then you are about to make an extraordinary evolutionary jump in self awareness. You are about to become aware that:

**Life is Motion.**

**All things move.**

**God is All Things.**

**God is That Which Moves.**

**All Movement is Change.**

**God is, therefore, That Which Changes**

**You are One with God**

**You are That Which Changes**
**All Change is Creation**
**You are That Which Creates**

Here is that piece of elementary wisdom which you must accept if you are to recreate yourself in the image you choose. It is perhaps the most important point made in *Conversations with God.*

Now you may think that you already know this. You may think that we have taken many pages to bring you to a place with which you are already familiar. And perhaps you *are* familiar with this concept. Yet you may not be familiar with its *implementation*, for if you were, you would not be reading this book; you would not be seeking that which you already have; you would not still be trying to find the way. You would *be the way.* And you would be showing the way to others.

(*"I am the way and the life. Follow me."*)

So let us agree that we are all still seeking to remember these great wisdoms, and let us always see the value in revisiting them, especially when they are put in a new way in which we can understand them more clearly, so to move closer and closer to total implementation, total awareness, total acceptance, total expression of Who We Really Are.

A major factor, then, in re-creating yourself is understanding and accepting that you have the power to do so.

Again we say, you may consider this to be somewhat elementary; that you, and perhaps even large portions of society, have gone way past that.

Yet there are many organizations, movements and even religions which teach just the opposite. These groups say that your only hope is accepting that you are *not* able to recreate yourself, that you are *not* able to change; that you are, in fact, *powerless to do so.* (Alcoholics Anonymous is such a group.)

In their sort of reverse psychology, they teach that your only hope is acceptance of your hopelessness. In their topsy-turvy paradigm, your greatest strength is supposed to be acceptance of your greatest weakness.

By creating such a paradigm, these organizations and churches then produce a need for something or someone *else* to be your Strength. By admitting, acknowledging and accepting your utter powerlessness, you obtain the "power" (from another source) to change what you want to change.

Interestingly, this having-it-all-backwards philosophy has actually worked for some people. And to that degree, one supposes, it has value. But only very limited value, for it proposes a very limited view of the Self. And in the long run, in the larger mosaic, *that view can never be empowering.*

The reason it has worked for some people, perhaps many, is that many people – perhaps most – find it much more comfortable to believe that they do *not*, and *never did*, have power over their own lives. The comfort in this is in concluding that they are therefore not responsible for the way things are.

For some people, if they cannot find comfort in the way things are, they can at least find comfort in the fact that it is *not their fault.*

And, of course, it *is* not their "fault." As *Conversations with God* points out, it is not a question of fault, it is a question of choice. You are where you are because you *choose* to be. Things are the way they are because you *choose* for them to be.

(A much more detailed discussion of this is contained in CWG. A particularly powerful pronouncement is found in *Book One*. Many references may be located by searching under "*Choice*" in the index.)

The first step toward changing anything is accepting your own role in creating it to be the way it is right now. That is step one.

# Acknowledge Your Self as the Creator of all that you wish to ReCreate.

**EXERCISE #1**

Do the following exercise on the next page. List five things about yourself and your life as you are now living it that you'd like to change, or recreate in a new way:

1. ____________________________________________

2. ____________________________________________

3. ____________________________________________

4. ____________________________________________

5. ____________________________________________

Please do not read right past this exercise and fail to do it. Remember, you picked up this book because you wanted to *recreate your self anew.* We are starting that process. And the first step is picking up a pen and filling in the blanks above...or, if you think you may want to pass this book on to someone else, make up your own list on a separate sheet of paper. But *do it.*

Good. Now make a second form on another piece of paper, or use the format provided here, and in the left hand column, rewrite your list of five things you'd like to change, and in the space to the right, explore and explain to your Self *what you did* to create that which you'd like to change.

1. What I'd Like to Change... ____________________

   What I did to Create it like it is... ____________________

   ____________________

   ____________________

2. What I'd Like to Change... ____________________

   What I did to Create it like it is... ____________________

   ____________________

   ____________________

3. What I'd Like to Change... ____________________

   What I did to Create it like it is... ____________________

   ____________________

   ____________________

4. What I'd Like to Change... ____________________

   What I did to Create it like it is... ____________________

   ____________________

   ____________________

5. What I'd Like to Change... ____________________

   What I did to Create it like it is... ____________________

   ____________________

   ____________________

Remember now, you are not seeking to change or to recreate events, or even circumstances, through the process which you are undertaking in this book. We are seeking to recreate *yourself.* That is, Who You Are, and Who You Choose to Be, in relationship to the people, places and events of your life as you have experienced them thus far.

You *cannot change the events themselves,* nor can you change *any past circumstance.* That is because a thing once created cannot be destroyed.

What you *can* do is *recreate your present experience of them,* and, in fact, your present experience of anything at all – including your*self.*

Now in the last exercise, under "What I did to create it like this," you may have written in :

"I don't know." Or, "Nothing at all."

If you wrote "I don't know" in Column 2 next to any item in Column 1, go back now and look at that again. Erase or cross out "I don't know" and ask yourself...what would I write if I *did* know?

Write that now.

This is a serious part of the exercise, not a joke. It is a process which we use in our ReCreating Your Self workshops with great success. So we really want you to do what the paragraph above requests.

If you have done it, you may find – as many in our workshops have found – that you know more than you think you know about why things are the way they are. Still, if you continue to come up with "I don't know," address the "Self" as if it were *another person*, and say to your Self: "I know that you don't know...but if you *thought* that you knew, what would your answer be?"

Allow the Self to then quickly reveal the answer...and write it down as fast as it comes to you.

You may be surprised at this process and how powerful it is – particularly if you take the suggestion to literally "talk to yourself" as if your "self" were *someone else.*

People are often shocked at what the Higher Self can reveal when the Lower Self (for lack of a more eloquent term) detaches from Its own prior thoughts, feelings, and expectations of Itself.

This is called Divine Detachment. It is when the Lower Self steps away from the Drama it has created and allows the Higher Self to observe and comment upon it, clearly and without emotion; honestly and without hesitation; completely and without reservation.

You will know this process is working for you because there will be no negativity, no judgment, no anger, no embarrassment, no shame, no guilt, no fear, no recrimination or sense of being made wrong – just a simple statement of what is so. And that statement may be very illuminating.

So open yourself to receiving that statement. Allow yourself to Know. Then, as you look at what you Know, and as you explore and examine the choices you've made in your life thus far, make an honest, quiet, open assessment of whether you'd make those same choices in the future.

Yet understand that you cannot even hope to make changes in your life – to recreate yourself anew – unless and until you are able to accept complete responsibility for every event that's occurred in your life so far.

You must...

**Acknowledge Your Self as the Creator of all that you wish to Recreate.**

Now this may be the most difficult part of the process, because to acknowledge yourself as the creator of your experience means, for many people, placing yourself at *fault.*

That would be a huge mistake, but for many it may seem a very logical place to go. They will look at some of the experiences in their life and they will ask, "Now why in the world would I have wanted to create *that?*" Then they will recriminate against themselves for having been "so *dumb,*" or so "naive." Or they will become angry with themselves for creating and re-creating (in a seemingly never-ending pattern) the very experiences they say they are trying to avoid.

Some people who fall into this trap may even become self *haters.* That self hatred sometimes (probably often) leads to self sabotage, which can lead to self *destruction,* or destruction of virtually everything that is meaningful to the Self – relationships, careers, health, any possible chance of success....

It is one of the most dangerous Traps of the New Age. That's what I call them, because they are exactly that, and you have to be very careful of them. They are mental boxes you can get yourself into by accepting certain New Age aphorisms as Truth, with only limited understanding.

Statements such as "What you resist persists," "For every door that closes, another opens," or, "You are the creator of your every experience," are typical of these New Age aphorisms, and such statements can lead to weirdness if, before you start living them as Absolute Truth, you have not come to deep understanding.

(Complete Understanding will, of course, bring you to Ultimate Awareness that there is no such thing as Absolute Truth...which will eliminate the problem altogether.)

And so I try to warn people before they move much further into this process of Re-creation that accepting *responsibility* for the events in one's life does not mean accepting *blame* for them. "Blame" can in any event be assessed only when something has gone wrong, so in your life blame is invalid because in your life *nothing has gone wrong.*

Nor has it in anyone's life.

Life is perfect, and it is when we see the perfection that all blame, all anger, all hurt, all sense of damage and loss, victimization or guilt for the victimization of others, disappears. God hasn't created imperfection, and Life *is* God. Therefore, Life is Perfect, as God is Perfect, and our challenge is merely to see that Perfection. "See the Perfection" is, however, nothing but another aphorism if we do not seek to embrace it, too, with deep understanding.

Failure to see the Perfection in our lives or in the lives of others is merely failure to see what the Soul is up to. Remember that the Soul – which is your direct link to Infinity – is here on a mission, and that mission is Evolution.

The Soul is seeking to create and to experience Who and What It Really Is, and It will use any tool, any device, any encounter, any experience It feels may be useful in the creation and the expression of that. No Soul can be acted upon by another against It's Will, and no Soul can act willessly.

That's a new word, and I've just made it up. It is the opposite of *willfully*. The reason it is not a word is probably because nothing can happen that way, and there was no reason to have such a word.

Willful behavior is possible. Willess behavior is not. All behavior is willful; that is, comes out of our willpower. The statement, "You have no willpower" is *always false.* What is more accurate to say is that "you do not have the will to stop this." Now *that* is *true.* If you *had* the "will" to do something (that is, if it was your will to do so), *nothing could stop you.* For Will is everything, and as *Conversations with God* teaches, your Will is God's Will. Therefore, it is true, what your Mother used to say...

**Where there's a will,**
**there's a way.**

You must try to understand this, seek to grasp the fullness of its meaning, because when you do, you will also see that Everything Is Perfect, for everything arises out of Will, and everything in *your* life arises out of *your* will.

The Great Masters understand this totally. They Know in Completeness. They *grok.*

That is why Jesus said, when his followers raised their swords to stop him from being taken by soldiers to his trial and crucifixion, "No! Do you think I cannot now call upon legions of angels to put a stop to all this if I wanted to? Think you that any of this is happening to Me against My Will? Do you imagine that I am powerless here; that I am without willpower? I tell you, it is the very power of My Will which is *causing* this."

Then what, you may ask, is the meaning of Christ's other well known utterance: "Not My will, Father, but thine" – ?

Here again, all truths must be held in deep understanding, and with Completeness.

In this case, it was Christ who also said, "I and the Father are one." This means that his will and God's will are *one and the same.*

What was happening, then, on the Mount of Olives when Jesus spoke these unforgettable words? The Master was going through a moment of weakness, just as we all do, in which He imagined, for just a moment, that all that was happening to Him was not of His (God's) choosing. He imagined, for just a moment, that His will and God's could be different. His prayer in the Garden of Gethsemane is an earnest declaration of Jesus' willingness to nevertheless meld His will with God's; to surrender to God's Will, which He *knew* to be One and the Same with His Own when He was in a clear state of mind.

Not only was it Jesus who said, "I and the Father

are one," it was also Jesus who said, "All ye are my brethren."

If we take Him at His word, then we, too, are "one with the Father," and our will, too, is God's Will. We can only escape this conclusion by pronouncing Jesus a liar.

Anyone care to make that pronouncement?

Having come to a new understanding of our own role in the creation of our experience, the second step in the Re-creation Process is to finish all of the "unfinished business" which our old understandings created.

(If you are still having trouble reaching this new understanding and this new level of acceptance of your own role in the creation of your life as it is, please reread *Conversations with God*. Also, you may find the audio cassette, *The Bend Talk,* available from our Foundation, extraordinarily eye-opening.)

This process of completing your Unfinished Business is incredibly important. I call it the American Express of Transformation. That because you don't go anywhere without it.

Let's look, then, at...

# Finish your unfinished business.

Before you were aware of the role you have played in creating your own reality, you may have had a tendency to blame and project anger onto others whom you have seen as being pivotal to the creation of many of the sadnesses and hurts, losses and disappointments in your life. If you have not been extremely diligent, you will by now have created a memory bag full of people and events which you hold in your consciousness as having damaged you.

This bag is your Unfinished Business. Lugging that bag of trash around with you is what has slowed you down on your trek towards Enlightenment. It is what has made it necessary for you to stop and rest so often on your journey to God; on your Trip Back Home.

It is what has kept the full measure of Love from your life, and the full glory of Who You Are out of your experience. For it is a Principle of Life that you cannot experience Who You Are so long as you are experiencing others as who They Are Not. And so long as you make another the Villain, the Persecutor, the Instigator and Cause of your pain, you say the lie about that person – and thus about yourself. You must therefore pay attention to...

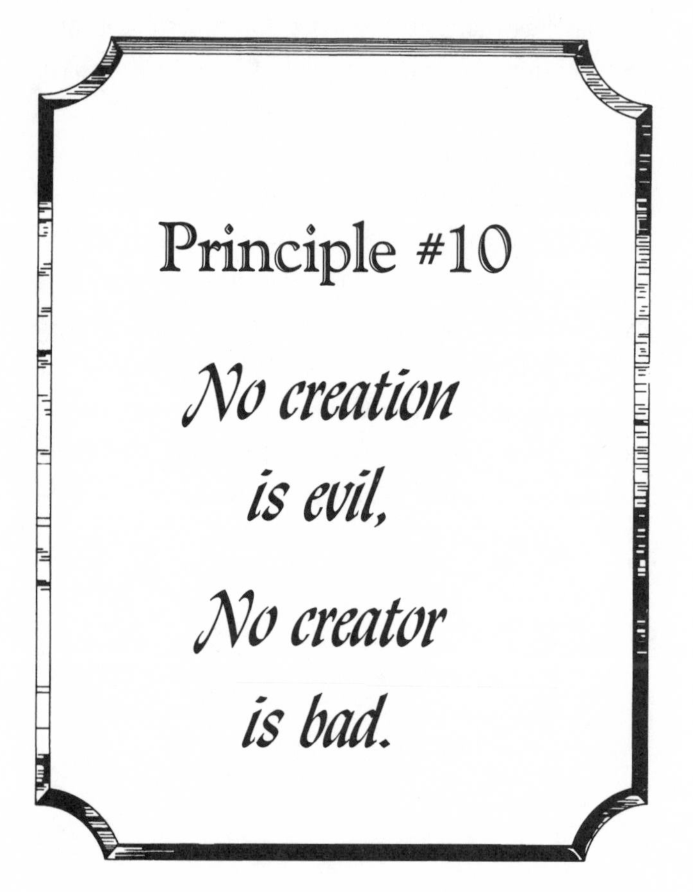
Principle #10
No creation
is evil,
No creator
is bad.

A thing is only "evil" because thinking makes it so. As *Conversations with God* points out again and again, it is your *thought* about a thing which gives that thing (person, place or event) its meaning.

Now, having a thought which says a certain thing is "evil" is not necessarily "bad." In fact, it is by what we, each of us, call "good" and "evil," "okay" and "not okay," that we define our Selves, and decide who we are. Yet we must always remember that we are forming the definitions *ourselves*; making the decisions ourselves. Contrary to popular opinion, this is not work that God has done for us.

The beauty of this is that while we are going around deciding what is important to us, we can also decide what is not important. While we are deciding what is evil, we can also decide what is not evil. While we are deciding what is painful, we can also decide what is not painful.

Many people have learned how to control physical pain in precisely this way. There are not a few people who can get into a dentist's chair and undergo an entire procedure without feeling a moment's discomfort. Some of these people call this "mind over matter." And they are correct. What they have done is simply *decide that the dental procedure is not painful.*

Using exactly the same tool, we can *decide that an emotional experience is not painful.* The death or departure of a loved one, for instance, need not be a cause of pain – though for most people it obviously has been. The experience of being betrayed, or abused in some way, need not necessarily be painful or damaging – though, again, for most people it obviously has been.

The truth is, these occurrences in and of themselves are not painful; not even evil. They are simply what they are. This brings us squarely, and rather quickly, to...

# Principle #11

*Nothing matters, nothing has any meaning at all.*

Life is meaningless. The only meaning it has is the meaning we give to it. Likewise, individual experience, individual occurrences, individual happenings, and other individuals themselves, have no meaning whatsoever save the meaning we give them....

And the meaning we give them is most often not related to what we are actually *experiencing*, but rather, to what we have been *told* should be true for us.

Nowhere is this more apparent than in our experience of God Herself. For instance, because we have been *told* that God is a "He," we have come to *accept* that God is a "He," and we have come, many of us, to not even question that. Yet is it possible that God is a "She?" Or that God is neither? Are we coming to our conclusions about God based on our *experience* of the energy we call God? Or based on something *somebody else told us?*

Similarly, we have been *told* that God is a jealous God, a vengeful God, a God who will punish us horribly and without end if we do not obey His commands. Yet everything we experience inside of us tells us this cannot be so; that these are not the qualities of Godliness. Still, many of us look past our own inner experience to the outer world and the teachings of others. They must be right, we say. After all, what do we know?

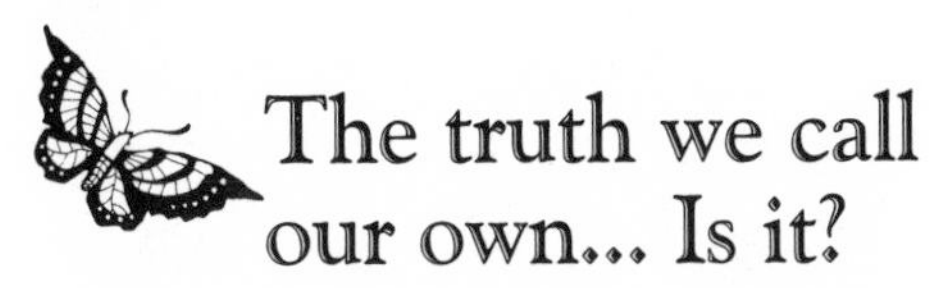

## The truth we call our own... Is it?

We make this mistake of looking right past our reality to the doctrines of the world in other matters as well. It is largely the prior experience of *others* which drives our own experience. It is the teaching of others which creates the Truth we call Our Own.

Yet even listening to our *own* prior experience is not infallible, for even what *we* thought about a thing before is not our true teacher, because our prior experience...*and the way we experienced it*...was based on the teachings and the experiences *of others*. In truth, we have experienced very little of Life purely, without adulteration, without contamination, without infection from another.

An example:

Most children take delight in their own body (because their *experience* of their bodies is *delightful!*) until they are taught by the outside world that to take such delight is wrong; that to flaunt such delight is inappropriate; and that to actually invite such delight is sinful. A child knows *instinctively* that there is nothing in the world to be ashamed of regarding the body until that child is taught that *not* to be ashamed *is shameful.*

These "teachings" then become the truth of our children, even though they are in direct conflict with the experience of our children, thus creating in many of our children inner turmoil for the rest of their lives.

## Our mangled perceptions abound

And it is by no means the realm of human physicality and sexuality to which this mangled perception is limited. In virtually every area of our lives, our judgments (and therefore our decisions) about things have been at the very least colored, and in many cases totally shaped, not by *our* experience, but by the teachings, truths and doctrines of others.

Usually these "others" (parents, relatives, teachers, friends) are well meaning – yet that renders their announcements and teachings no less inaccurate, merely non-malevolent. The truth is, these others cannot know what our experience of a thing is, they can only know about their own. They should, therefore, be disqualified to act as judge and jury of ours. But judge it they do...*and we let them.*

Not only do we let other people judge us, we actually *live by the judgments they have made.*

It is only the strong who do not. It is the individual who is his or her *own person* who does not. It is the ReCreated Person who does not.

If you are not yet a totally ReCreated Person, this book invites you to become one. And the second step in that process is to finish your Unfinished Business; allow yourself to let go of all the interpretations and "teachings" of "others" about the experiences *you've had*, and decide for yourself what they did, and now do, mean in your life.

Now let me give you one example of what this kind of freedom can bring.

Not long ago, a woman came to me in deep sadness and frustration because she could not seem to maintain a warm and loving relationship with her husband. One of the big problems was that she had lost her sexual desire for him. Even though she knew and acknowledged that he was a good man, that he never did anything to hurt or harm her physically, and that he was never sexually inappropriate in any way, she could not find a place of sexual desire for him. And she couldn't figure out why. It was not boredom, it was not that he had put on tons of weight or lost all his hair or anything so superficial. In a way, she told me, she wished it *had* been one of those things. Then, at least, she could *understand* it.

Closer exploration of the whole topic of this woman's sexuality revealed the source of the problem. She had been sexually abused as a child. Repeatedly. By a relative (not in her immediate family).

But wait. It wasn't as simple as you may be thinking, for her "turn off" with her husband was not because a man had abused her as a child, and she therefore wanted nothing more to do with sex. Quite the opposite. She had actually *enjoyed* being treated sexually as a child – and it was her *conflict* at having found it enjoyable which produced her present difficulty.

The conflict arose in that, while *she* did not have the experience of *any damage whatsoever* as a result of her childhood sexual encounters, she received the message, sometimes directly, sometimes indirectly, *that she should have.* This did not square with her *experience*, but she had nowhere to go with that. It was even worse, really. Because on the few occasions when she felt safe to acknowledge that she did *not* feel she had been damaged, not only was she told that, well, she *should* have been damaged...she was told as well that she probably *was* damaged by all this – *and just didn't know it.*

She was made painfully aware of the "horror" of what this man had done to her, and, in women's support groups, as well as with counselors to which she had gone for help, she had been told how *angry* she should be about all this – and how angry she *would* be if only she really knew how deeply damaged she was.

In fact, she was told, she had been so deeply damaged that she *didn't even know it.*

Once, when she bravely announced to her group that she was *not* angry and could *understand* with *compassion* (while not condoning) the awful need and the terrible illness and the inappropriate and criminal behavior of this man, she was told that she was repressing her anger, and that she should learn how to express and release her rage.

She tried it for awhile, but it was always an act, always a shallow performance. Deep inside, she was simply *not angry.* She even wondered, deep inside, if she might have actually played a role, by clearly enjoying what was happening at the time, in encouraging the man to continue.

When she revealed *this* to her group, she was told that it was dysfunctional to take responsibility for this man's inappropriate behavior. And while that statement might have made some sense within the parameters of dysfunctional systems theory, it made no sense at all within the parameters of her own *experience.*

As we've already noted here, it was not what occurred, what she did, in those encounters with the older man that caused her to feel shame. *It was the fact that she did not feel bad about it, that she'd actually enjoyed it, which produced the shame.*

There was also another point of conflict. This woman wanted to forgive the man who had abused her; to let *go* of the negativity she had been told for years that she was supposed to be feeling. She had been blessed with a deep understanding. And when understanding comes, anger departs. She knew perfectly well that her experiences were not age-appropriate and were a crime against childhood innocence by her male relative. But still she could not be angry. Sad, perhaps. But not angry. Why? Because she knew too much to be angry. She had far too much compassion, far too much understanding of the foibles of the human condition to be angry. She had forgiven her older male relative long ago in her heart. The second reason she could not be angry was that she had enjoyed the sexual experiences herself way too much to try to pretend now that those were among the darkest hours of her life.

They simply weren't.

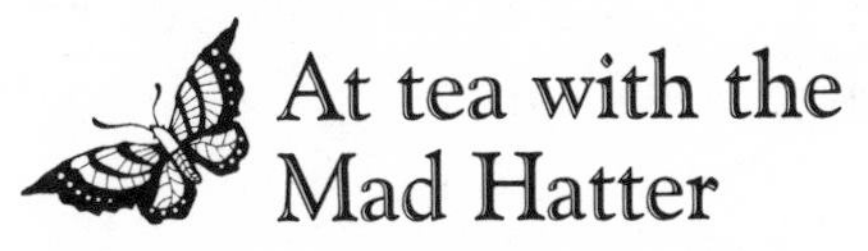

## At tea with the Mad Hatter

Yet – and here is the irony – it was *others* who made it difficult for her forgive and forget, look at the situation philosophically, and live without shame. Like Alice having tea with the Mad Hatter, she found her "reality" denied, invalidated, made wrong. And so, to make things "right," she'd made an unconscious decision to *never again* enjoy what she had once enjoyed "wrongfully."

What is amazing is that through all the counseling and all the women's groups, not one person ever said to her the obvious: that it was perfectly understandable she might enjoy the sexual attentions of her older male relative, perfectly natural that she might respond to the stimulations, and not at all "wrong" or "shameful" that her body reacted in this way.

As long as she felt it was "wrong" for her body to react positively, openly and eagerly to sexual stimulation when she was young, she would *never* allow it to do so as she grew older.

What changed everything for this woman was her finally learning that it was perfectly *natural* for her body to react to her older relative the way it did, and *perfectly all right* that she had enjoyed that reaction.

This new point of view rearranged her thinking on her own sexuality dramatically, and gave her permission to revisit her childhood encounters with the older man from the framework of *her own experience,* rather than what had been told to her, or what she felt was expected of her. She allowed herself to release at last the years-long feelings of shame.

She soon found that she was more able, in the moments of present-day sexual encounters, to *stay with her experience*, rather than retreat and return to her constructions of her childhood experiences – constructions built mainly on the reactions of others, not on what was *actually going on.*

I have used this real-life example, and taken a good deal of time with it, because I think it dramatically illustrates how we attach the meanings of others to experiences which are our own.

Now I do not mean to suggest or assert by this example that all childhood sexual abuse is non-damaging, nor that such abuse is, in any degree, the fault of the child, nor that because a child may enjoy the physical stimulation and the emotional and psychological attention, this makes the experience "right," or "not so bad." I am not seeking to make any of those points.

The point I am trying to make, in fact, has nothing to do with sexual abuse. That's just what was involved in this particular case. The example was simply an illustration of how our Minds can create our Reality – and how what we think can so easily be influenced by what others think, or what others say *we* should think.

It was an illustration of how quickly and willingly most of us move from our *experience* to our *judgment* (usually based on someone *else's* judgment) of a person or event. And I wanted to show that, in truth, nothing matters at all, except that which we *cause* to matter, out of *our decision about it.*

Now, another exercise. These exercises provide practical tools with which to apply what you are hearing here. To get the most out of this material, do not simply read through them, or turn past them.

### EXERCISE #2

Please take out a sheet of paper now and create a list headed: the Five Most Impactful Negative Experiences of My Life.

Good. Now consider the list carefully. Make sure you've chosen the five worst, the five most negative. If it is painful for you to bring these to mind, go through the pain and do it anyway. Or better yet, *decide that the exercise is not painful.*

Now, beneath that list, and on the same sheet, write down what happened. I mean, *what actually happened* within this negative experience. Not how you felt about it, but what actually *occurred.*

I'll give you an example, by making just such a list here.

**THE FIVE MOST IMPACTFUL NEGATIVE EXPERIENCES OF MY LIFE**

1. *My wife's announcement of her pregnancy by another man, and her intention to have his child*
2. *My cousin's death in Vietnam*
3. *My 17-year-old daughter's battle with cancer*
4. *My brother's suicide*
5. *My father telling me, when I graduated from the Marine Corps training camp at Parris Island, "I never thought you'd make it."*

**WHAT ACTUALLY HAPPENED DURING THESE EXPERIENCES**

1. *My wife said words to me which I didn't like. A week later, we separated.*
2. *My cousin left his body.*
3. *My daughter underwent extensive surgery and could have died. She did not, and has survived over 20 years.*
4. *My brother left his body at a time and in a manner he selected.*
5. *My father said words to me which I didn't like.*

Okay, there's my two-part list (a composite of the real life experience of some people I know). Now make your own.

When considering the second part of the list, be sure to look at the events which actually occurred, not at how you allowed the events to effect you. For example, if you had as Item 1, "My father yelled at me about my grades once in front of all of my friends," you might well write in part two of that listing: "I was so embarrassed I wanted to die." Yet what I want you to write in section two is simply a description of what actually happened. In this case, you might write: "My father raised his voice and said private things to me in the presence of my friends."

You get the picture? Don't remember how you felt about it, simply write down what actually occurred. How you felt about it *is the part you are making up.*

Go ahead, then. Write out your five-item list.

Terrific. Now we're going to conduct a little experiment. I want you to make a third list, headed THE RESULT OF WHAT HAPPENED.

Look at the items on the first two lists, and now make an honest assessment of what resulted from what actually happened. (Not what resulted from how you *felt* about what happened. These may be two different things. Just look at how things have turned out ultimately.)

Got it? Good. Try not to look at the next page until your list is complete. When you've finished making your entries, compare your third part to our own completed Part Three on the next page.

I arrived at our Part Three by actually interviewing the selected friends from whom I drew these examples, asking them to describe the long term results of their experiences. Realizing that these were highly impactful occurrences, I asked them to be as objective as possible.

I found it interesting to note that these results were in every case positive. That may not necessarily be your situation, but it was in these instances. Let's take a look.

## THE RESULT OF WHAT HAPPENED

1. **In some ways I think I love her more now than I did then. I have learned to love her unconditionally. And in my own life I have found a freedom that I never knew when I was with her.**
2. **Life went on. I made some decisions about using war as a means of resolving differences; when**

**it was okay and when it was absurd.**

3. **I came to value my relationship with my daughter, and it has blossomed.**
4. **I came to understand more completely human pain and the depths to which it can reach, and I determined never to make judgments about others which could cause them pain. I have valued life more than ever.**
5. **I learned to live with my father's opinions and thoughts about things, even when they did not agree with mine. I learned that I was not "my father," but that I was Me. And in giving my father the space to be who he was, I came to love him without condition, allowing us to be very close when he died.**

The purpose of this exercise was to allow you to see how the final result of an experience is more often caused by our thought about it than by the experience itself.

In fact, this is always the case.

In and of itself, no thing matters. What causes it to matter, and the way in which it matters, is our idea about it, our thought about it – and that idea is either based in our actual experience, or in our warped perceptions.

Finishing one's Unfinished Business becomes easy when one realizes this. We see the enormous truth in Walt Kelly's wonderful observation, made through his comic strip character Pogo:

*"We have met the enemy...and they is us."* We see how we have been our own worst enemy.

## The role of Truth Telling

The next step in finishing our Unfinished Business is to tell the truth to everyone about everything we know about that.

There are Five Levels of Truth Telling:

1. Tell the truth to yourself about yourself.
2. Tell the truth to yourself about another.
3. Tell the truth to another about yourself.
4. Tell the truth to another about another.
5. Tell the truth to everyone about everything.

Strive to rise to the Fifth Level of Truth Telling as fast as you can. Tell the truth to everyone about everything. This is an astonishing way to live, and it is a major step in re-creating yourself. It requires fearlessness, but not rudeness; courage, but not insensitivity. For fearlessness is not tactlessness, and courage is not a social blunder.

You will finish with your Unfinished Business once you tell your truth about it, *whatever* that truth is.

To finish your Unfinished Business, make a 3-part list of *all* the major negative events of your life, just as you did with the top five. That list may take some time to make – you may want to do it over a period of a few days – so give yourself all the time you need.

When you have made the list and finished the work, look to see what this brings up for you. Now, on a separate sheet, write the names of any people you feel you have "unfinished business" with about any of these things; one name per page.

These people may be living presently in the body, or may have made their transition from this Earthly experience. It doesn't matter. Just write their names; one name per page.

Now, underneath each name on each page, complete the following sentence:

*What I'm afraid to tell you is...*

Finish the statement truthfully, honestly, and completely.

Now pick up the next page and do the same with the name you find there. And keep on completing these statements for every person whose name came up, each on a different page.

Good. Now, if the person to whom you addressed the statement is living in the body, *give them the paper on which you wrote.*

If you do not feel you can do that, ask yourself why not. Are you feeling unsafe? What do you think would happen to you if you felt the fear and did it anyway? What outcome are you seeking to avoid? Has it profited you to keep avoiding this outcome in the past? How would it feel for you to simply tell this person the truth? Would it be freeing? What are you afraid would happen if you were free from living this lie?

This is what we mean by finishing your unfinished business. You cannot make any real progress in re-creating yourself unless and until this work is done.

Now if the person whose name you wrote on the page is no longer in the body, you have a chance to do some inner dialogue work with that Beingness.

Find a spot in your kitchen, family room or living area where you can set up two straight-back chairs. Place the chairs about three feet apart, facing each other. Put yourself in one chair, and mentally place the person to whom you have written in the other.

This is a mental "game," but do it anyway. Just sit quietly in your chair for a moment, imagining what it might be like if the other person were also really there. When it feels right to do so, say "hello" to this other Beingness, welcome them to the room, tell them you've thought of them in this unique and special way because there is something you would like them to know. Then read them your statement; the one which began, *What I am afraid to tell you is...*

As soon as you finish the statement, take stock of how you feel. If you are "feeling" or "sensing" what you think the other person might now say, move immediately to the opposite chair, look back to your Self in the chair you just vacated, and say the words *for* them!

When you feel you've said exactly what they want to say right now, return to your own chair and respond.

Keep this "dialogue" going as long as it feels good to do so. Notice how you feel when the process is over.

This is called Inner Dialogue. It can be a marvelous process, and is sometimes most effective when undertaken with another person present. Find someone who loves you, who can understand the process and what you are trying to accomplish.

And what *are* you trying to accomplish? You are seeking simply to get some feelings out, to move through some truth, to express some important thoughts, to say something that needs to be said – and needs to be heard. And is the other person, the person to whom you wrote the original note, really hearing what you have to say?

*I believe the answer is yes.*

Yet the question is irrelevant, because the benefit is derived whether it's all just a "mind game," or whether there really is dialogue between souls going on.

There are many others ways, as well, to "finish your Unfinished Business." Workshops, retreats and seminars abound. Programs, lectures, sermons, books...the world is filled with tools and opportunities, and this work *can* be accomplished.

When it is, you will be so refreshed, so refilled, so revitalized and so renewed that you will surely wonder what took you so long, and why you waited until you did to *get on with things already.*

And that will lead you to...

## Decide what is true for you now.

The process of re-creation is a *decision,* not a *discovery.* That is, it is not something we find out about ourselves, but something we choose for ourselves.

It can be difficult to make these new choices when we are encumbered by our old thoughts, our old ideas, and our old mental constructions about the past. That is why is it necessary to finish one's Unfinished Business. Once this is done, the space is opened for us to fill with a new creation, a new idea, a new concept of Who and What We Are.

No longer do we have to keep operating out of..."I'm unlucky," or "I'm ugly," or "I'm not nice," "I'm always victimized" or "I'm not worthy." At last we can come from "I'm WONderful! I'm powerful! I'm magnificent!" And even, "I'm the cause of my own experience, and every experience I have given myself was perfect for the creation of Who I Am and Choose to Be right now."

That is a very empowering statement. It is a statement which removes us from victimhood and from being at the effect of life, and places us in the space of pure creation.

It is the beginning of Re-creation.

We have reached the moment of pure creation when we realize and declare that we have *always* been at that moment, in every time of our life.

It is not necessary to understand *why* we have created what we have created, why we chose to experience particular life encounters in certain ways. We did, and that is that. Stop questioning yourself about it. Stop asking why. The question "Why?" is the most irrelevant question in the whole human adventure. It is meaningless, pointless, fruitless, yielding nothing but more questions with equally pointless answers.

There is only *one* question of any value, of any worth, of any importance at any given moment: What do I choose now? That is all that matters; that is all that counts. The answer to that question is the key to your future. It is the fuel which drives the engine of your experience. And remember, *not to decide is to decide.* For not to make a *specific* choice is to choose whatever life brings you. And that's not very self empowering, is it? So now, let's enter into another process. Please take out the piece of paper you used for Exercise #2, and use it again for...

## EXERCISE #3

Examine carefully the Five Most Impactful Negative Experiences of Your Life. Read the statements you wrote in Parts 2 and 3 for each of the five experiences. Now, for each of Numbers 1 through 5, *decide Who and What you choose to be Now with regard to that.*

For instance, if you were sexually molested or raped as a child, and that is one of the five items on your list, decide Who and What you choose to be *now* with regard to that experience. Do you choose to be angry? Do you choose to be sad? Do you choose to be suspicious? Do you choose to be sexually frigid? Do you choose to be dysfunctional in your relationships? Do you choose to continue to feel victimized, and to live from Victimhood? Do you choose to be healed? Do you choose to live from understanding, compassion, forgiveness and love?

What do you choose?

What do you *choose?*

Make the following table, and fill in the blanks:

| Negative Event | What I Now Choose to Be with regard to that | What I *used* to Choose |
|---|---|---|
| | | |
| | | |
| | | |
| | | |
| | | |

Now make some decisions and fill in the second column. Your New Self will arise out of these decisions, so make them carefully; make them deliberately; make them consciously. That is, with Full Consciousness.

See if there is any difference between what you now choose, and what you used to choose, with regard to these top five negative events.

If there is a difference, see if there is any shift in your quality of life over a period of time out of your new thought about that.

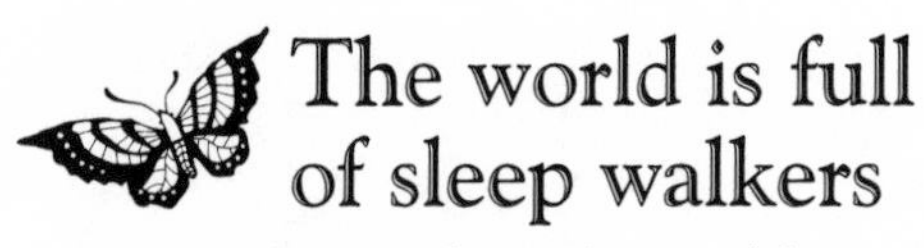

## The world is full of sleep walkers

So many people in the world are walking around unconsciously. You can see it on their faces at the mall. Lack of consciousness. Lack of interest in anything having to *do* with "consciousness," or the "consciousness movement."

Often, these people look like the walking dead. There is no smile on their face. There is no bounce to their step. There is no energy in their body.

It is very sad to see these people. Yet the biggest sadness is that they don't even know what they are doing to themselves. People have so much lost touch with their feelings that they often don't even *know* –

are not consciously *aware* – that they are truly unhappy (much less why).

Not many years ago a woman came to one of my classes. She looked hard as nails. Her brow was deeply furrowed, her eyes were ringed with darkness, and her lips were tight and pursed. She did not laugh during the first 40 minutes of the class. She did not even smile. Finally, I said to her, "How are you tonight?"

"What do you mean?" she asked, suspiciously.

"I mean, are you happy? Are you a happy person?"

"Yeah, I'm happy," she allowed. "Well," I said, "you ought to tell your face about it."

I invited her to smile, lighten up a little, put some brightness behind her eyes. This woman was so unhappy, she did not even know she was unhappy. Unhappiness had become such a way of life with her, it seemed *normal.* People who appeared outgoing, fun-loving, cheerful and open seemed *abnormal.* She actually *thought* of them as "abnormal."

She looked at such people (I learned later) and wondered what they wanted; why they were putting on such an act, and how they could fake it so well. It was a real astonishment to her to find that most of these people were *not* putting on an act, wanted *nothing* from her, and couldn't have "faked" such genuine warmth and *gemüchlichkeit* if they tried.

One of the reasons that so many personal and spiritual activities today are said to be part of the "consciousness movement" is that it is out of *conscious awareness* of what is going on with us that changes, alterations and improvements are made.

## Principle #12

*Conscious choice creates new consciousness.*

*New consciousness creates new experience.*

All experience arises out of Consciousness. All consciousness arises out of wakeful choices. If we are to recreate ourselves we must stop the sleep walking and walk in wakefulness. We must live in awareness. We must move to a new level of Consciousness.

## Extend your choices into the future

Once you choose *what* of yourself you now wish to experience with regard to the past, extend those choices out into the future. That is, decide *now* Who and What you Are, and Who and What you *Choose to Be*, with regard to not only the events which *have* occurred, but events which are *about* to occur.

What's that? Impossible, you say? Not at all. And, in fact, this is the last step in Re-creation.

# Decide what *will be* true for you in the future.

Something that is not widely known or under stood is that you can *select ahead of time* the moods, reactions, responses and experiences *you are going to have* in your tomorrows. Just as you can decide before sitting in a dentist chair that "this is not going to hurt," so, too, can you decide in advance of other experiences just what they will be for you.

You can choose these responses and reactions deliberately and willfully, and with such resolve that nothing can shake you from them. In the moment you do this, you become not only the master of your own destiny, but a master of Life itself.

What's ironic about all this is that, as illustrated in the dentist example above, we all *know we can do this.* There is not a one of us who has not done exactly this – namely, decide *ahead of time* how we are going to feel about a thing – and yet, for reasons that are not very clear, we refuse to apply this already honed skill to the majority of the moments in our everyday life. Quite to the contrary, we choose and use this extraordinary skill rather sparingly, employing it on perhaps half-a-dozen to a dozen occasions *in a lifetime.*

This observation leads to a life-changing question:

**What would happen if we employed this skill every hour of every day of every year, all our lives?**

The answer is, of course, that we would seldom, if ever, experience a moment of pain, a moment of anguish, a moment of bitterness, anger or frustration. Our lives would be in perfect order, and we would know it, because we would have *caused* them to be so.

The *events* of our lives may not necessarily change; conditions may not get any better, but our *experience* of those events will change forever.

Ultimately, we will not repeat such moments at all, *for we will have mastered them.* We will have learned to *welcome* them; to appreciate and bless them as the grandest gifts from the greatest creator; gifts which allow us to be, express, experience and fulfill Who We Really Are.

The irony is that, having learned to welcome such moments of what we would formerly have called mayhem and negativism, they will go away, for *what you resist persists*, and *what you look at disappears.*

In this way, you will have recreated yourself (and your experience of life) anew.

Thus, our final exercise in this book may be its most powerful one. Here it is.

## EXERCISE #4

Make a list of Future Experiences you imagine that you are likely to have. Obviously, you cannot predict all of them, but there are probably a few you *can* predict; that exist as possibilities at least.

For the sake of the exercise, start off with a few obvious ones. Take a look at the first two or three on the sample list drawn up for you below...

### SOME EXPERIENCES I COULD POSSIBLY HAVE IN THE FUTURE

Getting cut off in traffic

Having a spat with my spouse

Losing someone I really love

Being confronted with loneliness
Not having as much money as I'd like

Now, next to each item, make a notation of the new experience you now choose to have in those moments, should they occur.

Look at this list every day as a reminder of the new choices you have made. Remember, what you resist persists; what you look at disappears.

As you confront the experiences you predicted you might have (or something close enough to them), remember the choices you made regarding how you're going to experience the moment. Then insist with your Self upon experiencing it that way.

This is called *Mastering the Moment.*

As you master more and more such moments, expand your list of possible or probable future events and episodes, and again make conscious choices as to Who and What You Are, and Wish to Be, with regard to those adventures.

When you encounter the moment you predicted, remember the choices you have consciously made and move into the experience of that.

## And if you fall back into old habits and old patterns?

If you do not succeed in recreating yourself anew from top to bottom in one day or one week or one month, do not be discouraged. Be persistent. You may find yourself falling back into old patterns and old behaviors in the face of some of the encounters you predicted you might experience. If you do, simply notice your choice – *and choose again.*

Don't make yourself wrong for this. Refuse to judge yourself. Simply notice the choices you are making...and choose again.

*Keep choosing the*
*Greatest Version of the*
*Grandest Vision ever you had*
*about yourself.*
*Keep choosing what God would*
*choose. Stay conscious,*
*keep awake, and move*
*to the next opportunity to*
*ReCreate Your Self Anew.*

And especially do not be discouraged if life begins to "show up" in more and more difficult ways. For the moment you make a choice about Who You Are and Who You Choose to Be, everything unlike it will come into the room.

That is because you cannot be Who and What you Are except in the space of that which You are Not.

You cannot be thin if there is no such thing as fat. You cannot be tall if there is no such thing as short. You cannot be big without small, cool without warm, nor anything at all without its opposite number. This is explained in detail in *Conversations with God*, and again in the book *Bringers of the Light.*

So know and understand that you can *expect* such difficulties. Indeed, they are and will be your greatest gifts.

Go now, and reach deeply within your imagination, there to find the new idea you have about yourself. Place that idea into your experience; create it as your new reality. *ReCreate yourself anew in the image and likeness of God.*

In this will you have fulfilled your destiny. In this will you have done what you came here to do.

## The Steps and Principles in this Book

Principle #6: *Life is motion.*

Principle #7: *All movement is change.*

Principle #8: *Perspective creates reality.*

Principle #9: *All change is creation.*

Step 1: ***Acknowledge your self as the creator of all that you wish to recreate.***

Step 2: ***Finish your unfinished business.***

Principle #10: *No creation is evil; no creator is bad.*

Principle #11: *Nothing matters. Nothing has any meaning at all.*

Step 3: ***Decide what is true for you now.***

Principle #12: *Conscious choice creates new consciousness. New consciousness creates new experience.*

Step 4: ***Decide what will be true for you in the future.***

A closing note:

Opportunities for more experiential work with the concepts and principles found in this book are available through the ReCreation Foundation created by Nancy and Neale Donald Walsch, principally through its 5-day intensive retreat, ReCreating Yourself, offered four times yearly, and facilitated by Neale.

Schedules for these spiritual retreats, attended by people from all over the world, are available from the Foundation upon request at 541-482-8806 or visit our website at www.conversationswithgod.org

ReCreation

*The Foundation for Personal Growth*

*and Spiritual Understanding*

PMB #1150
1257 Siskiyou Blvd.
Ashland, OR 97520
(541) 482-8806
Fax: (541) 482-6523
email: recreating@cwg.cc
website: http://www.conversationswithgod.org

Millennium Legacies, Inc., MLI,
publishes books, audio and video tapes, music CDs
and other materials agreeing with and advancing the
message of the *With God* series of books authored by
Neale Donald Walsch.

Our cost of writing, producing and distributing this book is approximately $3.25 per copy. Your price is $10. We provide this information in the interests of transparency.